MY BROKEN Heart

Poems of Love and Rejection

SALIM KHALIL HADDAD

authorHOUSE

AuthorHouse™ UK
1663 Liberty Drive
Bloomington, IN 47403 USA
www.authorhouse.co.uk
Phone: 0800.197.4150

Published by AuthorHouse   01/17/2019

ISBN: 978-1-5462-9871-7 (sc)
ISBN: 978-1-5462-9872-4 (hc)
ISBN: 978-1-5462-9870-0 (e)

Print information available on the last page.

This book is printed on acid-free paper.

CONTENTS

Dedicated to my dear sister, Leila.

PREFACE

These poems are about fitful unrequited love and unfulfilled desire. This is common in the experience of men and women, but I wrote in verse because it affected me. The poems are in chronological order. Each tells of my emotional condition at the time of composition.

I loved a woman intensely and asked her to marry me, but she refused. She promised herself never to marry after her husband died. For several years, I did my utmost to make her change her mind, but I failed. Later, she broke her promise and married another man. The poems were initially addressed and given to her soon after the time of writing, except for those that were written after she broke her promise.

My Broken Heart

My broken heart, my broken heart.
She hit it hard; it fell apart.
She will not mend it, though she can,
For only she can cure each part.

My broken heart, it feels the pain
Since it was mangled, torn, and slain
By her, whose love, beyond compare,
Enslaved it with my will and brain.

My broken heart, it cannot heal,
Though it can beg and crawl and kneel
And fail to live without her love—
But falter, splinter, cry, and reel.

My broken heart does weep and wail,
And love beyond the human scale,
And long and pine and yearn each day
More than the drunkard for his ale.

My broken heart, it fails to cope
When, in the dark, I search and grope
And cannot find the thing I seek—
Oh, this hell! There is no hope.

Without You

Without the soil, the seed will die.
Without the sun, dark is the sky.
Without water, life is no more.
Without the air, no bird can fly.

Such is life without you with me,
Like dead branches upon the tree—
Harsh loneliness, full of sadness,
When joy and gladness run and flee.

And in the turmoil of each day,
My sick heart begs of hope, a ray,
That perhaps you will change your mind
And then come home to me and stay.

Oh, that would be the biggest prize,
Which any man would idolize:
The lasting love that will not die
But flourishes and multiplies.

You

I wake at night and call your name.
Your image quickly fills my mind.
I see your body and your frame
And count you best in womankind.

Your face, for years, has thrilled indeed
My longing soul and aching heart,
And made my searching mind concede
That beauty filled you from the start.

But now I hug and hold you tight,
And press you hard against my breast,
And feel your heart beating with might
And pounding hard against my chest.

How much I love you? None can know,
None can discover or construe.
No one can know or even spell
The feelings that I have for you.

You are the sparkle of my soul,
More precious than the earth, more fine,
More wonderful, gentle, and whole.
And may I dare to call you mine?

The Beloved

The bright red rose speaks of true love;
Her smiling face outshines the rose.
And oh, how gentle is that dove,
The one I followed and I chose.

I set out to gain this treasure,
Not knowing that my heart will break
And feel a pain of great measure
With no relief for my heartache.

Now her person is my delight.
It pushes all the gloom away
And kindles in my soul a light
That she will be mine, mine one day.

The sun uttered, "I too am fair."
The moon responded, "So am I."
But she is fairer than the pair
And all the stars in the night sky.

Wonderful woman, lovely, rare,
Who in the whole world can match her?
She is unique, beyond compare—
Her face, her eyes, her lips, her hair.

It has become my happy lot
To love this woman and adore.
To give her all that I have got,
All that I am, and much more.

Stay Close beside Me

Stay close beside me; say nothing at all.
Let me taste the pure nectar of your lips.
Listen to my heart and hear its loud call.
It calls for you; it runs and never trips.

I would embrace you hard and not hurt you.
I would regard you the most precious thing.
I would love you with love, tender and true,
And let my soul hold fast to you and cling.

Is there a greater joy on earth for me
Than to be with you and feel your affection?
Than to know that you will remain and be
My love, my delight, my satisfaction?

How much I wish that all the clouds will scatter,
That straight before us is the open sea,
That obstacles will die out and shatter,
And there is nothing left but you and me.

You will always be the throb of my heart,
My great desire and longing of my soul.
My model of perfection and my chart,
The one with whom I reach my happy goal.

Stay close beside me always; be my wife.
I will dearly respect and honour you,
And you will be ever my joy in life,
Greatly more wonderful than the vast blue.

The Red Rose

O winter rose that blossomed red
In the dark alleys of the night,
You sprang and gave life to the dead
By your grand and beautiful sight.

When the soft breeze blows upon you,
And the dew of heaven comes down,
I caress your petals, and oh,
In love's turmoil I swim and drown.

In the beauty of the springtime,
When new life enriches the land,
You grace the scene in every clime.
You remain beautiful and grand.

Love, oh love, how deep and steady,
Growing fast as the days go by.
Gripped by the red rose and ready
To suffer for her and to die.

O red rose, my heart is ravished.
Your fragrance adds to my delight.
Be not surprised or astonished;
Your pleasures rapture and excite.

A Tale

The old king said to his minstrel,
"Sing to me a little story."
He said, "I sing of a damsel.
It's sad, but has its own glory.

"Once upon a long time ago
Lived a woman in Celtic lands.
She was of rare beauty and so
Pure, virtue fell from her fair hands.

"By pure chance, one day he saw her,
Instantly fell into the trap,
And felt his heart float in the air,
And his strong will and power snap.

"She lived high up upon a hill.
He was a man, tender from birth,
And her beauty inflamed him still.
She had no equal upon earth.

"One day he dared to seek her mind
To ask if she would think of him,
For he told her in words most kind
Her love had filled him to the brim.

"He offered her all that he had—
Himself, his marrow, and his bone—
And said that he would be most glad
To make her his own wife alone.

"For strong reasons only she knew,
She was not willing to accept,
And her determination flew
In his sad face; he left and wept.

"He went about from street to street,
Lonely, dejected, and forlorn,
Unwilling to talk or even eat,
Ruing the day that he was born.

"In a short time he went away.
People wondered if all was well,
But they found out one gloomy day
That he died on the spot he fell.

"The people said love had killed him.
His love was beyond his control.
They sang for him a solemn hymn
And prayed that God would keep his soul."

Such Love

My days are empty without you.
The hours are wearisome and long.
The night is dark and lonely too.
Oh, how love flares and remains strong.

I sit and stare through the window,
Hoping to see you passing by.
I must endeavour to let go
Such wants, such hopes, and let them die.

In the hours of each new morning,
In the business of the day,
In the night and in the evening,
I think of you along the way.

Will such love, such pain, such passion
Remain unrewarded, alone,
And grow old, hoary, and ashen,
Beheld to moan, beheld to groan?

I would the earth quivered and quaked,
The sun no longer gave its light,
Than that true, wondrous love forsake
Or let that deep love die one night.

Your Love

Restore to me some ray of hope,
That which you have taken away.
Let me no more in darkness grope
But spring out to the light of day.

May it not be a hope given
To reduce the anguish I feel,
But rather hope by truth driven
To comfort and solace and heal.

Let the sea roll on forever.
Let each river pursue its course.
But keep my heart; do not sever
Its lasting love from its pure source.

Let the free birds sing their dawn song.
Let the fox cubs wake up and play.
But do not tarry for too long
To make me yours one happy day.

Love has triumphed; it did vanquish
My heart and made of me a slave.
Do not let me die or languish.
I will love you until the grave.

Do Not Ignore

As much as vital is the air
For live birds in the sky,
So is the great love which I share;
Without it I would die.

As much as dolphins, fish, and whales
Need water in the sea,
Without your love, my life will fail;
Its end few men will see.

Without the soil, seed will not grow—
The plant, the shrub, the tree.
Such is my life will slip and go;
Deprived of you, will flee.

Out of the womb, he cannot thrive.
The foetus is no more.
Likewise, my life will not survive
If such love you ignore.

I Will Never Let You Go

Come to my heart; stay forever.
It is hard to perceive or know
How much I love you, and never
Will I think of letting you go.

As the rivers flow to the sea,
As the birds fly home to their nests,
So does my heart hasten to be
On your bosom, where it can rest.

Lovely woman who has held me
In your soft arms and squeezed me tight,
Oh, the bliss—who taught you to be
A flame that came into my sight?

I hold you in my arms, and oh,
What joy, what rapture, what delight!
What made you full of pleasure, so
Ready to inflame and excite?

You take first place in thought, in time.
I like your love more than pure gold.
It is most wonderful, sublime.
I want to keep you and to hold.

I cling to you with all my power,
Constrain you that you will not go.
I wish you with me every hour,
Observe your smile, see your face glow.

When the night comes home to beckon
That we must part, be on our way,
How I wish that you would reckon
To be mine from that very day.

You Passed My Way

You passed my way,
Broke my poor heart,
Then went away.

Love has indeed
Deceived me well,
Left me to bleed.

How can you be
So hard, so stern,
Cruel to me?

How can you think
To make me walk
Close to the brink?

You surely can
Make up your mind,
Destroy a man.

My fault, I knew:
My only fault
Was I loved you.

You would not see
How much I wished
My wife you'll be.

I would give all—
My life, my goods,
The great, the small.

Would not deny
A thing you need,
But satisfy.

Could you not tell
How hard I fell
Under your spell?

That I loved you
More than myself?
And that is true.

Did your heart mind
I found you best
In womankind?

You made me feel
Best of all men,
Proud, but genteel.

I walked with pride,
Holding your arm
Close by your side.

You held me high,
Enchanted me,
Then let me die.

You made me lose
My dignity,
My will abused,

And let me fall
Upon the floor
To taste the gall.

As for today,
You grabbed my heart,
Threw it away.

You thought that I
Would let you go,
Let you slip by.

But all the same,
I love you still
And call your name.

I cannot find
Words to show how
You filled my mind.

Can I say more?
My body, soul,
You they adore.

Is there relief
However short,
However brief?

Is there no cure
That will remain,
That will endure?

There is no lack
Of a sure cure;
You hold it back.

Said to yourself
That one must be
True to oneself.

And made excuse
That you your oath
Will not abuse

No matter how
I beg you to
Rescind your vow.

That awful vow,
Which is the cause
Of trouble now.

Why are you bound
By words when I
Was not around?

It makes no sense;
It took its toll
At my expense.

Nor would you tell
How you threw me
Quite close to hell,

And would cause pain
To one who learnt
Not to refrain.

Nor to believe
Your conduct will
Cause him to grieve.

No, to my mind,
You always were
Gentle and kind.

What have I done
To lose the prize
That I thought won?

O wretched man,
I just exist:
An empty can.

Perhaps I should
Go far away,
And that for good.

I will lament
A treasure lost
By your intent.

Perhaps be seen
Mourning each day
What could have been.

Best let me die
Than live to make
That bitter cry.

You passed my way,
Broke my poor heart,
Then went away.

The Flower

The fairest of flowers is she,
Red rose as lovely as can be
Spreading her fragrance all around,
Refreshing all, enchanting me.

A man passed by along her way
And fell to her charm right away.
And when he dared to pick the rose,
He bled as thorns pierced him that day.

He wore it close to his own heart
With pride and zeal right from the start.
Could not see in the people round
Beauty, as in her every part.

And then he clasped her by the hand,
And on the wind he was to stand.
For he quite soon did realize
There was none like her in the land.

I Loved You

I loved you with a love that's true,
A love that every day is new,
A love, fresh as the morning dew.
This is how I loved you.

A love that will never grow old,
A love more precious than pure gold,
A love that is fearless and bold.
This is how I loved you.

And if they said to me, How great?
Is it as strong as severe hate?
I say, As high as heaven's gate,
This much have I loved you.

And if they said, Will you forget
How love will make you grieve and fret?
I say that I shall not regret
If at all she loves me.

Bring all that makes men glad and see
It is but a drop in the sea—
The sea that held me and will be
Love forever for you.

She Said

She said, You cannot know or tell
How you will be in future times.
I said, You must learn fully well
My love is constant through all climes.

She said, In due time you will shake
Your feelings and will change your ways,
I said, I will never forsake
Loving you till the end of days.

You cannot judge aright and say
That such love will just age and dry.
For once I fall in love, I stay
In that sure ground until I die.

This, my nature, is really me;
Pattern of my life will not change,
It is stable, will always be,
No matter how you find it strange.

Just grant me some more time to prove
That my resolve is great, sincere;
That nothing can take or remove
My earnest love for one so dear.

You Said Goodbye

While happy, you cast me aside;
There was no point to heed my pride.
But like a little upset child,
I simply cried and cried and cried.

I am a grown-up man, mature;
Thought that I'd learnt how to endure.
But when you said to me goodbye,
I felt helpless, wretched, and poor.

If they said, Plague has struck the town,
Or, Young Joe fell and broke his crown,
It would be nothing to compare
With the despair dragging me down.

If only things were otherwise
And you are not a treasured prize,
But normal woman of your kind
And not a goddess in disguise.

Then I would dare and wish and hope
That with my feelings I would cope,
And not desire what could not be
Beyond my strength, beyond my scope.

Such is the irony of life:
What is wanted is really rife,
But hard to find, harder to get,
Whether it be treasure or wife.

Even so, I give my right hand
To have my hungry wish to stand,
To make you mine, whom I adore,
The one most precious in the land.

Closer To You

As ivy clings to the trees
I cling to you.
As whales swim the open seas,
Free in the blue,
My soul knows just where to find ease:
Closer to you.

So let me be at your side
With naught between.
Let me in your big heart hide;
There let me lean.
Let me walk with you with pride,
By all be seen.

When loneliness drags and wails,
The day is bleak;
When life feels as if the gales
Will shout and shriek;
When rain floods valleys and dales,
'Tis you I seek.

When you are far, a few feet
Away from me,
I ache with every heartbeat
Closer to be,
Until I rest beside your seat
Happy and free.

Being with you is desire
Born of the heart.
Living without you is fire,
Will always smart.
Life is wanting, not entire,
With us apart.

She

When seagulls wake
And the waves break
Upon the shore,
I will awake.
My heart will ache
For her once more.

I try to still
My soul and will,
But then I find
That she is still,
Always will dwell,
Deep in my mind.

And when the sun
Has fully run
Cardigan Bay,
She and no one
Has truly won
Myself today.

Second to none,
No trait to shun,
Blonde in her hair;
She has outdone
Just everyone
By her sweet flair.

With the moon bright,
High up at night,
I miss her charm;
I wish she might
Perceive my plight,
Give me some balm.

She takes full sway
By night and day
On heart and soul;
Please find a way
And come to say
I make you whole.

Unattainable

Plead and try as you may,
Beg of her every day,
It is of no avail.
She will not change her mind,
And you will sadly find
That your efforts will fail.

Watch your heart crack and break,
Crush all hope and forsake,
For there is only pain.
Do not sigh, do not groan.
Learn that you are alone,
Helpless, mangled, and slain.

Do not aim for great heights;
Rejection burns and bites,
Is unexplainable.
You are no longer free;
You agonize, but she
Is unattainable.

A Final Plea

Sally,
Save my heart from destruction,
For none other can.
A heart sick with affection
In a lonely man.

O greatly loved and longed for,
Grant him his request.
You watched him beg and implore
With pain in his breast.

Bestow love and happiness
To a tortured soul
In passionate readiness
To give you his all.

The Vow

It was taken when earth was grey,
After disease snatched him away
And left his wife and children there
To miss him and bemoan the day.

Then in the solitude and calm,
She vowed that she would not cause harm
To other men who might one day
Fall to her beauty and her charm.

She did not think that time would bring
A man to love her and to cling
Like moss upon the barren wall
And count himself rich as a king.

And then, in time, he too went bust:
His wife died and was laid to dust.
In due course, he approached the one
Who stole his heart and won his trust.

Her own words stood between them now;
He felt dismayed he had to bow
To something spoken long ago
To herself in the form of a vow.

He thought it wrong that she should make
A promise that she could not break,
Not knowing that in future days
Someone would give all for her sake.

It is not right to limit days
And set a hard pattern that stays
By a past pledge made to oneself
That treads on what one feels and says.

The present day is something new;
The past must not kill it or spew,
Or refuse what it has to give
When he comes to love her and woo.

Come Back

The tender kiss, the lovely smile—
'Tis what I miss, though for a while.
Beautiful face looking at me,
Charming embrace, strong as the sea.

And now you are away from me,
A distant star. What can I be
But a poor wretch longing for you,
A lonely sketch a master drew?

Come back and find how I missed you;
You filled my mind and my heart too.
I smell your hair and touch your face
When you are there, safe in my place.

I cannot tell why on this earth
I fell for you and knew your worth.
Woman who draws me to her side—
The one I chose, the one I eyed.

One More Time

O most loved woman in the world,
Be to me like a hummingbird
That sucks the sweetness readily
And still hovers, almost unheard.

Give me the thing for which I crave,
The thing for which my all I gave.
Let me not be lonely, deprived,
Failing to mend my heart and save.

But put the sparkle in my soul;
Then I will be like a young foal
Full of life's zest and energy,
Perfect, complete, not lacking, whole.

So will the nature of my days
Be like the sun, will shine and blaze.
And let all men around me say,
This man is most blessed in his ways.

The Photograph

I have found a photograph
Of me when I was young.
It seemed like a paragraph
That from my past had sprung,
Or like a short epitaph
That was by some bard sung.

I was youthful and handsome,
A sparkle in my eye.
Good-looking and wholesome
With nothing to decry,
With life's joy in my bosom,
Which none could stultify.

The years had blossomed for me;
God gave me a good wife
And saved and protected me,
Secured my afterlife.
To him all the praises be
Now and throughout my life.

As I thought on the likeness
Of mine, radiant and smart,
I wondered how such brightness
From my soul did depart.
Now, old and in the stillness,
I nurse my broken heart.

I Searched for You

I dreamt a dream that midst the crowd,
I searched for you but could not find
The one I love, as if a cloud
Shrouded you and left me behind.

My heart's desire was too intense
To glimpse you, but I could not see
Your lovely face, my recompense,
And I felt like a refugee.

It truly shows I yearn and long
For something which I cannot get,
And doomed to spend all my days long
Aching until my sun will set.

I wondered and reasoned and thought,
How can I ever be complete?
And with sorrow I searched and sought
To find a way to bear defeat.

You burn my heart with flames of fire,
And yet without you life is lame,
Devoid of hope, full of desire
Will you be mine and take my name?

Sally

Sally, the woman I relish;
The person I adore, cherish;
Whom I seek, for whom I languish;
The one for whose love I anguish.

The beat of my heart, its beauty,
The joy of my soul and booty;
Of whose passion I am guilty;
To whom I offer my fealty.

The day is bright with you only.
The night without you is lonely.
Life away from you is mainly
Halt, rising to run, but vainly.

Upon you is my fixation,
And without you is starvation.
Hard are the days of privation.
Are they not close to damnation?

The years have not dulled my passion
Nor robbed it in any fashion.
It is stout in its formation
And still burns without cessation.

She Is

The one on whom, when ill, I depended.
But her love broke my heart and not mended.
She is fair like a flawless diamond,
Like morning dew, most pure and unblended.

Too deep into her love I descended;
More of her fairness I comprehended.
When I asked her, Why are you so lovely?
I am nothing special, she responded.

The story of my life has not ended.
I think daily on whom I befriended.
Though she said, I will not marry again,
Lest I make you upset and offended.

My hapless tale cannot be amended;
I neither kept my pride nor defended.
I still struggle on, hoping that somehow
I will accept the fate I contended.

Do Not Forget

Do not forget me when I am away.
Think of me tenderly each passing day.
Think of me lovingly at evening time,
Of our days together in summertime.

I miss you when distance sets me from you.
Love's desire has greatly flourished and grew,
Has flowered like blue hyacinths in the spring,
Sped towards you like bluebirds on the wing.

Will our hearts go cold? Will they really burn?
To which of these two options will they turn?
There is no doubt to where my heart will go:
Seeking after you, burning with a glow.

You have managed to turn me upside down
From my lowly feet to my head and crown.
How can I forget you? How can you be
Distant from my mind, a stranger to me?

May the days roll on quickly and recede.
May nothing stop my return or impede
That I may hug you eagerly and show
How much I love you, as you truly know.

Travel

The train is at the station,
Getting ready to go.
I feel my heart's pulsation;
My legs are weak as dough.

I am going without her
To a distant land.
It is not what I prefer—
An awful thing to stand.

I shall use my memory
Of her, which I retain,
When I am solitary
And sitting in the train.

But then the plane will take me
To a land far away,
And with my own kindred be
During my long, long stay.

Remembering and longing
For her as days go by,
With potent desire gnawing
To see her eye to eye.

Cold Turkey

I felt bereft without you; I now tell
That Cold Turkey does not remove the spell
Of wanting you, for it miserably failed
And left me lovesick, feigning to be well.

So much for old tricks. Is there nothing new?
Can anything make me not think of you?
Nor remember you in every event
While those around me never had a clew?

But there is a comfort in the blue sky
That quite soon I shall be ready to fly—
Not with my own wings, but in a jet plane—
And return home to see you by and by.

I Tried

I told you of my love and tried
To accept what you would decide,
With strong hope surging as a tide,
But found that you rejected me.

It is my fault I could not cope
When my great love and my great hope
Crashed down into a dreadful slope
Of rejection that destroyed me.

The world was beautiful and bright
With many a fine, splendid sight.
It's henceforth grown as dark as night
Without a light to comfort me.

I know that you have reasons why
You should not join with me and try
To have my love until I die,
The love for one who enchants me.

I found you are beyond compare,
With whom I could all life's joys share,
But now all I can do is stare
On you who always excites me.

You Conquer

I do not know where you have learned
To vanquish men and conquer hearts
And make them seek with their minds turned
To your alluring body parts.

You show desire then turn away
Until a man stands helpless, lost,
And cannot find a proper way
To retrieve heaven at all cost.

Then he discovers ruin, doom
Have turned to be his property,
That grief and sorrow do consume
His thoughts and steal his liberty.

Oh, how I try hard to redress
Destruction that befell my soul
And wish that somehow I possess
Ability to gain control.

Such is my case, I cling to you.
I would give all to gain your hand.
I hope and wish you will undo
The chains that I find hard to stand.

You Withdrew

You passed my way for a short time.
You gave me joy at wintertime
And spring, but then at summertime
You decided to leave me.

You deprived me of love that warms
My loving heart and then transforms
Its substance to withstand all storms—
A love I miss acutely.

You passed my way, fragrant flower;
I was delighted for one hour.
In one flash, a sudden shower
Washed out our close bond to sea.

I think about the days, now past,
The days that failed to stick and last,
When a small thing became a blast
Destroying what we had built.

Wail now, oh, wail with me how things
Turned out to be a bag of strings
And flew like a blackbird on wings
With ailing souls left behind.

My Aching Heart

My heart is aching badly,
More than I can describe.
It will not rest, and sadly
No drugs found to prescribe.

I tell it to quit ailing;
Will not listen to me,
It keeps on daily railing,
"I'm wretched as can be."

O wretched heart, what ails you?
Where has joyfulness gone?
"Her love, deep as the vast blue,
Made me truly undone."

Is there a cure to purchase?
What would you have me do?
"Her love is really matchless,
But one day she withdrew."

I miss, I miss the pleasure
That I had by her side,
I love her beyond measure
And there is none beside.

Time

I have lost her; woe is me.
Who can lose a treasure?
She walked away, let me be,
To nurse love without measure.

As I fell in deep distress,
Seeing my whole world crumble,
She said, Time will heal the stress.
I knew my heart will grumble.

Is time my friend? Who can say?
Am I just a fatalist?
I know well that time this day
Is not a heart specialist.

Time, hand in hand with absence,
They say should ease my anguish.
There is no doubt in my conscience:
I shall just mourn and languish.

Great hurt comes with greater loss,
And nothing can mend it.
Life without her is but dross,
And this is the hardest bit.

Love

Love is described extremely well
In first Corinthians thirteen:
Stands firm against the gates of hell,
Its noble features seen.

It is not easy to provoke;
It suffers long and is kind,
For it is as strong as the oak
And to the main truth inclined.

This does not mean it feels no hurt;
It soon forgets, will not grudge.
Though upset by words, sharp and curt,
Remains faithful, will not budge.

It bears all things, endures all things
In a manner few men know,
And hopes and never fails, but brings
Humility that will show.

Such is my love for you, my friend.
Will not let obstacles stand
Along our pathway and offend
A relationship too grand.

So think upon me with your heart,
Do scatter ills far away,
Be to my life a vital part
And never leave me, but stay.

I Love You

I love you with great passion,
I love you with great zeal.
This is my true obsession,
And this is how I feel

You set emotions running
In an Olympian race,
For to me you are stunning,
The finest of your race.

When I am without you, far,
You are quite near to me.
In my thoughts you really are
As close as you can be.

Spark of my life and being,
The energy of my soul.
I'll love you till I'm dying;
You are my joy, my all.

Your Photograph

You grow older with dignity,
More beautiful each year.
You are free of malignity,
Too honest and sincere.

I glimpsed a photograph of you
Taken three years before.
And one taken this summer too:
It surely wins the score.

How did God make you beautiful
And give you such a smile?
The Almighty was too skilful;
To make you took a while.

More than happy with what I see,
Rather all excited,
I look on you with eager glee,
With love unrequited.

And then I bemoan my sad state
That you will not be mine,
However long I yearn and wait
For your favour to shine.

Enough

Enough of poetry—let go.
Oh, is it falling on deaf ears?
She does not will to undergo
A change of mind despite my tears.

So why describe feelings in verse?
It makes no difference to the case.
She is adamant and averse
To let me love her and embrace.

To love her in the rightful sense
And be at peace with what is done,
To be her support and defence,
Property of the chosen one.

So say goodbye to all my hopes,
Desires, and all my lust to be
A husband held by tender ropes,
Adoring her who sets me free.

I have grumbled and moaned too long.
I shall not bother or accost
Her soul, but resolve to be strong,
Regain the dignity I lost.

At Variance

You are trying to protect me,
But you managed to destroy me.
You are trying not to hurt me;
Instead you gave me untold pain.

Do you never feel a strong urge
To be loved fully by a man
And let your body with his merge,
Knowing there is no moral ban?

Do you think we cannot get on?
What better than love to cement
A bond that one time we had won,
But now has a trend to fragment?

Such is the case between us two;
We have reasons in plain conflict.
Mine may be right, yours may be true;
Whatever, I feel derelict.

Look upon me and be willing
To accept my compelling plea.
Your acceptance will be thrilling
And will restore the life in me.

My Words

Give attention to what I write;
They are not trash words that I say.
I speak of my life what is right,
Of how I truly feel each day.

I do not write just to make rhyme;
These are heartfelt emotions, pain.
From a deep pit I try to climb
To get my sanity again.

Think of each word, each feeling now,
How I express my present state,
And find a way to show me how
To take a loss that is too great.

There is a better way you know
Which can cure all my ills and pains.
So think of it, be kind, and show
You possess healing for my banes.

My Lot

All are ignorant of my plight.
They tend to think I am all right,
But they cannot know how I feel:
My heart cut with a sword of steel.

They say to me, Are you OK?
I answer happily and say
That I am absolutely fine,
Though in my heart I ache and pine.

Is life merciless and cruel?
Is it just a sparkling jewel?
Does it taunt us as not to give
What we wish to joyfully live?

Human life is a great ocean,
Restless and in constant motion;
Will not bestow what we desire;
Is heedless of sick hearts on fire.

I have been battered and denied
The happiness which exceeds all,
Which I pursued, for which I sighed
And found myself at a stonewall.

So will you now ask how I feel?
I cannot describe the torment
When wounded with a sword of steel;
Its cut can heal in a moment.

There Was a Time

There was a time when I was king;
I reigned supreme and unopposed.
But then life came with its sharp sting,
Saw I was beaten and deposed.

I had riches beyond compare
And wealth that few could dream about.
I then lost her just in one flare,
Lamented my fate with a shout.

I lost her and cannot regain
The ecstasy which I enjoyed.
I lost her and shall not again
Live in that love that was destroyed.

Lament my fate, lament my lot,
For life has been hard and cruel.
That left me helpless when it shot
From my hand a priceless jewel.

A Lost Cause

Trivial upsets manage to rule the day.
I tried, but I could not push them away.
They formed a strong barrier to obstruct
All that would pass along that happy way.

I deemed that you were love personified.
For you only I have hungered and sighed.
Fulfilment of desire, breaker of hearts,
For whose sure consent my soul ached and cried.

I left you with deep love within my heart;
It remained alive while we were apart.
And it must stay dormant and be as dead
Without hope to awaken my sweetheart.

I chased after you for more than one year;
Throughout each week you have become more dear.
I must let you go. You refused to be
A part of my life, happy or severe.

Despite what I said, despite what I feel,
I have lost the case; there is no appeal.
Just let me burn without any recourse
To someone to change my fate or repeal.

I shall soon return, for the time draws nigh
To look on your face with an eager eye,
See what I missed when I was far away,
Forget that I loved as the days go by.

The Thunderbolt

The field was ripe with luscious fruit
That made a most lovely scene:
Apples, oranges, and grapefruit
On trees beautiful and green.

But then there was a sign that said,
Do not trespass, do not pluck.
Go find some other daily bread,
Some other tame bird or duck.

He had to leave the field alone;
He was compelled to abstain.
Its sight and scent filled heart and bone
And were destined to remain.

This was amidst many a lake,
Amidst river and mountain.
He wished for what he would forsake
Of youth, the magic fountain.

Then later, what he feared most came:
A thunderbolt from the sky.
It crashed beside him, made him lame,
Then passed on quietly by.

It left a man in disarray,
Unable to adjure;
Attempting hard to find a way
In suffering to endure.

He said to himself, Such is life,
Is fraught with joy and sorrow.
It smiles one day, then pulls a knife
And blots out one's tomorrow.

Oh, must he to himself repeat
What wonders he now has lost?
Deprived of what makes him complete
And kept from snow and frost?

If things returned to what they were,
How happy he then would be:
A king, well dressed with charm and flair
And proud for all men to see.

The Walk

I walked along a lonely road,
Far from the house and my abode,
With thoughts of you.
They made my feet speed in flight.
Thoughts of you were my delight,
Lovely and true.

I prayed to God with every breath
To save me from this living death
If he saw fit.
You made your mind long ago
The marriage bond to forgo
And stuck to it.

God will not answer my prayer
Though it has reached his listening ear
Quite early on.
I know I must do his will,
Though it is hard for me still
That love lives on.

Oh, what a pity, what a waste
That you would not approach to taste
The love I give.
To live again and be free
From that which keeps you from me,
To really live.

In The Airplane

I touched her—oh, how soft her skin.
It set my heart aglow,
Reminded me of someone in
The town I love and know.

Oh memories, I love her so.
She brought me joy and pain.
Let me to your garden go
And see you once again.

There I will touch the one I miss,
Fragrant white English rose,
Feel on earth the ultimate bliss
Which no one truly knows.

Such are the daydreams that I see;
They do excite me well
And draw her much closer to me
Across ocean and swell.

Will You Remember?

Will you remember me when I am gone?
Have I been a passing phase in your life?
Will you remember the days, now bygone,
When I begged you and pleaded, Be my wife?

Will you think of days we spent together,
When I was as happy as a man can be?
When every smile you gave me did tether
My soul to your young soul, and you to me?

How I have lived my life in hope, yearning,
And cried for you in sharp and painful tones!
Lo, I have been very slow in learning
That you would never be bone of my bones.

I attempted hard to get over you;
I desired you and anguished. But I tried
To live without you, and nobody knew
To what extent I suffered, longed, and sighed.

Remember me in the stillness of night.
Remember me in the turmoil of day.
Consider that my years could have been bright
With you at my side, much loved each weekday.

Epitaph

She wounded me beyond telling
And left me there to die.
Beware if deep love is dwelling
In you as you pass by.

Beware, for her love will slay you
As hers surely slew me.
Beware, for her great power too
Kills—it truly killed me.

Left Apart

You left me to grow older still,
A lonely, disappointed man.
You made your choice; it was your will
To let me live the best I can.

The best I can is harsh and bare,
A great anguish of heart and soul,
With life reeling I know not where,
Without purpose, without a goal.

Is it written, is it decreed
That I should suffer till I die?
There is only one noble deed
That would succour and lift me high.

Some say I should accept my fate,
Not be a disappointed fool
That keeps knocking at a closed gate,
Unyielding as a stubborn mule.

Some say God wills that things should be
Exactly as they are, but yet
Love rages on; I fail to see
A way to make my mind forget.

Mourn my despair, lament my state,
Cry out aloud in agony.
Let rivers run and not abate,
For life is a sad irony.

My Stolen Heart

She made me destitute, bereft,
Wounded, bleeding, and raw,
And my beleaguered soul was left
Where sorrows bite and gnaw.

Is there relief, a sure relief,
For my grief-laden soul?
Is there some hope, however brief,
To retrieve what she stole?

She stole my heart, laid it aside,
And thought I would survive,
That in some way I would not slide
In sadness, but revive.

How poorly did she know my plight.
How little did she see
That stealing hearts will only blight
Strong souls beyond degree.

Now that my tale is told and done,
Tell her to do her part
That I may have that missing one:
My stolen feeling heart.

The Picture

I saw your fine picture unframed
On my computer and exclaimed,
You wonderful woman!
You made me feel a real man
As no other woman can.

Your power is mighty and grave.
You made my heart speed up and crave
For your love, proper and right.
You are smooth-skinned as the light.
You are Sally, my delight.

You let yourself into my head
And disturbed my sleep of the dead,
And energised me to long
With desire that is too strong
That you to me should belong.

Will you allow me to retain
What I was famished to obtain
Of that love, so rich and sweet?
Love that does not know defeat
And with vigour is replete.

Memories

Oh, memories, how sweet you are,
What joys you have brought to me,
Just like a bright light from afar
To let me glimpse her and see.

Oh, memories, painful but true,
You weigh heavily on me,
I wish she learnt, I wish she knew:
She is like a cedar tree.

Oh, memories of joys most real
With virtue and charm replete,
You know exactly how I feel:
She is my love, my heartbeat.

Oh, memories of joy and pain
Circling round me like a dove,
I visit you yet once again,
Painful memories of love.

Lament

Will she be mine? I cannot see
How this pure bliss will ever be.
I love her with body and soul,
And only she can make me whole.
Though in distress, I fully know
She determined it should be no.

Who would have thought that I would end
My life with anguish as a trend?
For in this world, there is one cure
Which none can obtain or procure,
For which I long, suffer, and yearn
Until Death says, It is your turn.

I lived a full and happy life
And dearly loved my darling wife,
But since I lost her, I felt bare
Without a companion to share
My innermost thoughts and desire
And love now flared up like wildfire.

And when I met this unique one
As brilliant as the morning sun,
I thought that I would start again,
Though she struggled to make it plain
That in this life I had my lot
And must not think of her, must not.

All well and good had she been like
Other women and not lifelike
With fragrant hair, emotive face,
A wholesome figure, full of grace
That came one day and set alight
My soul aflame with live firelight.

Now what I do is just lament
The way my last days will be spent:
In heart-burning and longing for
What will not be fulfilled before
I die and perish in the dust,
With my heart buried in earth's crust.

If You Loved Me

If you loved me twenty per cent
Of my love, then you would relent
Of some decisions you have made,
And our close friendship would augment.

How do you measure love today?
By meter or kilo you weigh,
Or feelings when one is entrapped
By how you look and do and say?

You cannot measure love by scale;
No human method can prevail.
It is something one knows and feels
And puts all else beyond the pale.

You might say, How do I love you?
My answer is easy but true:
I am willing to give my life
If events say, It is now due.

There is no greater love than this:
That man should enter the abyss
For friends treasured beyond compare
Without registering a miss.

Such is my love for you, my friend.
It has no borders and no end,
But hangs on every sight of you
To replenish itself and mend.

Oh, Sally!

Oh, Sally! How much I love you.
Oh, Sally! How much I need you.
Will you at any time be mine?
Will you love me as I love you?

Day after day, and in each night,
I call for you, struggle and fight,
Wishing that you were here with me—
Foundation of love and its height.

Tell me, why should it be that I
Should be afflicted till I die?
Wishing, hoping with no avail
That we may see with the same eye?

I feel towards you what I felt
For my darling wife, Jane the Celt:
Such raging love, such great desire
That was too grandiose and heartfelt.

We are at the edge of the brink,
So take the plunge and do not shrink.
Be courageous, and you will find
You are more precious than you think.

A Prayer

Help me to get over her,
O Lord, I cry.
Love is more than I can bear
Any way I try.

Please, I beg, I need your aid,
Your great power.
The memories do not fade,
They still flower.

Let me not think of her charm.
I was before
Content and serene and calm
And yet much more.

All the time, I think and see
With my mind's eye
What she can become for me:
A Mount Sinai.

Help me to get over her,
O Lord, I plead.
For she does lead me nowhere
Near what I need.

Is It the End?

Do you want to finish with me,
Presumably for my good?
Do you know me and clearly see
Better than I ever could?

After all that we had and shared
And remember for all time,
Will you throw it as if none cared
And count it not worth a dime?

Is separation best for me
Regardless of what I know?
My heart is as wide as can be,
As I was eager to show.

Should you finish, then so be it;
I shall not bother you more.
My heartache is mine, every bit,
Which nobody can restore.

Goodbye, love, forgive. I have been
A big trouble from the start.
I hoped joy would be mine to glean
Instead of a broken heart.

Sally Moods

When the sun is brightly shining
And a splendid day outlining,
It is a sign defining
That Sally's lips part in a smile.

When clouds gather in western sky
And shed their tears on earth, then dry,
The headwind gusts against the eye,
Then understand, Sally is sad.

When deer frolic amidst the trees,
Hares and leverets play with ease,
Various flowers maintain the bees,
Then surely know, Sally is glad.

Nature clothed with many a dress
Mirrors Sally in joy or stress,
As if she bids it with success
To show her feelings readily.

Tell Sally

Tell Sally that I love her.
Tell her that her like is rare.
Life is empty without her;
She is my love and my care.

As rivers run to the sea,
And planets circle the sun,
And flowers draw the honeybee,
Such she lures me like no one.

Tell her I am sick of love
And that by her enchanted,
She is to me like a dove,
A rose free and unplanted.

Forgive

Lord, you know I am heartbroken;
You heard me moan, be outspoken,
All to no avail.
I wish I could revert to be
My earlier self, my real me,
And no longer wail.

I used to relish what you gave,
Be it pleasant or be it grave,
Until all things changed.
I love her much, beyond compare,
But cannot convince her to share
What my heart arranged.

I should be joyful in you, Lord,
In your salvation and your Word,
But sadness prevails.
Forgive me for the task I find
Too hard when you are gentle, kind,
For my heart ails.

Forgive me that she is to me,
To my sad life, the only key
With nothing beside.
Come back to me and make me whole.
Revive my spirit and my soul.
Lay me not aside.

Show me your mercy, show your grace,
That I may be lustful to face
What comes my way.
Return me to myself before,
To sorrow and lament no more.
Do not answer nay.

The Night Cry

I wake at night, call out your name,
For you aroused in me a flame
Which no force succeeded to quench,
It burns unceasingly aflame.

What strong love, unfulfilled desire
Kindled my sturdy heart on fire,
Left me alone with no recourse
Only to hope and to aspire!

Oh, the deep irony of fate
When life with you, a dazzling state,
Has escaped far beyond my reach,
Crying, Soon, soon will be too late.

Will She Come?

I look through the window and say,
Will she come to see me today?
Will she really come?

Mine is a deep and earnest wish,
But my hope seems futile, foolish,
For she will not come.

And yet each day remains the same:
Pining for her, calling her name,
Hoping she will come.

Such is the pattern of my life:
Unending hope and inner strife.
All because I love.

What a Shame!

El Dorado is in sight;
I fail to reach it.
Heaven's gate is glistening bright;
I cannot breach it.
Lament my state, lament my life:
She refuses to be my wife.
What a shame!

What beauty God has made!
She came from his hand,
Far exceeding gold or jade
With no faulty strand.
But just like the forbidden tree,
One must not eat but only see.
Dare I taste?

Oh, what form before my eye!
What great urge to touch!
What alluring parts I spy
That stir me too much!
But all is lost; she shows no sign
That she will agree to be mine.
I am sad.

Man and Woman

When God's good creation took place,
He placed animals on earth's face,
Each kind with other kinds and space.

In God's image was then man made—
Best of creatures, of highest grade
And placed in a garden's cool shade.

But he felt incomplete, alone,
Till God made of his side, his bone,
A female who to him was shown.

Yes, of his side God did create
Woman to comfort, satiate,
To be his companion and mate.

I truly know how Adam felt
When he had by himself there dwelt
In that fruitful garden and belt.

He needed woman by his side
To be his partner, love, and bride,
And ever with him to abide.

A Woman Going Waste

A young woman going waste
Of softest skin, so velvety.
Let me love you, let me taste
That love of yours, a rarity.

Do not deny me what I crave,
What you refused me from the start.
Show me courage and be brave
That I be of your life a part.

You will find to your surprise
That life is beautiful and grand,
Rather than see my demise
At my failure to gain your hand.

Rather than be by yourself
And satisfied with what you are,
Lonely item on a shelf
Desired with love that knows no bar.

I Want to Go Home

"Why are you asleep, my dear friend?
I thought that you were fast asleep."
I want to go home and there spend
Time in my den, precious and deep.

I want to stay in there alone,
Think of ecstasy and gladness
That once were mine, but now have flown,
Leaving in my soul a blackness

So please let me go home and then
Arouse my poor soul from drabness.
For there alone in my sweet den
Lies the cure for all my sadness.

Tender Woman

Tender woman, sumptuous and true,
The very best of her kind.
Can you not see my love for you
As you inhabit my mind?

Search out its mountains and ridges,
Its chambers, caverns, and hills,
Its connecting roads and bridges,
And find that loving you thrills.

When a lonely bird is singing,
I remember your sweet voice,
As pleasant as church bells ringing,
For I loved you by my choice.

Think of me when you are lonely,
Of my zealous loving care.
Ah, you alone and you only
Can repair my heart or tear.

The Iron Gate

When the old iron gate squeaks,
My heart jumps at once and speaks.
She is now coming to see me,
But my alert mind recalls
That she at all times first calls
To see if I am at home, free.

I always yearn for that call
With my being and my all—
My waiting and my restless heart.
For I love to see her face
And be lost in her embrace,
Who sets me aflame from the start.

She is a beacon of fire,
Healthy and strong to inspire
My mind and be my unique goal.
So let me hopefully live
For what she chooses to give
That will relieve my ailing soul.

Alone

You will grow old and be alone
Without a friend to share your day,
Without the man whom you have known
Who loved you well when he was grey.

Will you recall how he pleaded,
Begged you to be his very own?
How you refused him nor heeded
The pain to which he became prone?

There will be none to hold your hand
As you journey along the road.
No one to comfort or to stand
With you when time hands you its load.

Perhaps a tear will wet your eyes,
Perhaps a feeling of regret.
Perhaps a choking and few sighs
Or some inkling of unpaid debt.

When I lay silent, dead and gone,
Buried beneath six feet of clay,
Desire will stop and be undone
As I enter eternal day.

I would have died sad, unfulfilled,
Taking my longing to the grave,
When my life was battered and grilled
With none to rescue, none to save.

What is now left for me to do
But to tend my wounds with sorrow?
You were my joy, but then you slew
Hope for today and tomorrow.

Remember Me

Remember me as the years are speeding,
Since I loved you, with my heart still bleeding
And yearning for some word of pure delight,
Saying to me, I am now acceding.

Each day brings me nearer towards my end
With hope abandoned and with none to mend
A broken heart that was once strong and free.
Remember me, remember me, my friend.

Remember what success I had in life,
How I faced problems when problems were rife,
How I became broken, haggard, and poor—
All because love has hurt me with its knife.

Remember me as the sunset draws near,
When I will wave goodbye to one so dear
As I journey to a far distant land
While the distance shortens year after year.

Remember me, with no trace left behind
But my poems, which were of constant mind,
Spoke of one topic again and again,
But never solved a thing of any kind.

Love Me

Love me, my darling, as you never did
Love any man before,
Except for your husband who is amid
The saints through heaven's door.

Give me yourself, and you will always be
The wealth that I possess,
More precious than all that could ever be,
More than I can express.

Love me, my darling; you will not regret
My love and care for you,
My heart and my love, my life since we met.
Let us be one, not two.

Your Lips

I find wild nectar in your lips;
It is fragrant and ever grips.
How many times I said outright,
"Try me, I can kiss you all night"?

Try me just once, and you will see
What loving passion comes from me.
Your lips turned purple will then tell,
I tasted heaven; all is well.

You say that it cannot be done.
Your words make me concede this one:
My saying shows intense desire
To kiss your luscious lips of fire.

The Cake—A Short Tale

Two English bakers liked to bake;
In time they made many a cake.
They said, We shall cook a rare one,
And in the process have much fun.
They measured an amount of flour
And said, It may take one hour.
All the ingredients were mixed in;
A finer cake could not have been.
So they placed it in the oven
With care—neither was a sloven—
Until the proper time had run
And the cake was perfectly done.
They said, This one will make a feast
For our noble guest from the East.
But by magic, the cake came out
A little girl, who gave a shout.
They said, She will grow, give her time,
Into a rare woman sublime.
Sadly, she will break a man's heart.
As for us, we performed our part.
No one can blame us when we bake
And make a very precious cake.

This is the story of the cake
Which the English bakers did make.

Pain

She is troubled by a headache.
Wish I could take her pain away.
I am troubled with a heartache
Which only she can take away.

Bodily torment comes and goes
With a slight echo that remains.
The ache of a broken heart grows,
Although at times it ebbs and wanes.

Can I endure bodily pain
And not endure an aching heart?
My head may hurt, my lungs may strain,
But my heartache tears me apart.

She Wrote

She wrote "with love", but would not say
"Love you" in words or line.
Nor did she once say to me, yea,
To let my being shine.

She showed restraint and was aware
That I would much rejoice
To hear four words, naked and bare,
Uttered by her sweet voice.

Using her words, "I soldier on",
Deprived of what could be:
A happy life with a white swan
Who means the world to me.

The Pyjamas

The evening and the hour draws
To signal the time for repose.
She wears pyjamas for the night;
Wish I could see that precious sight.

She must look alluring, entire,
An object of dreams and desire
That tell a man to forsake all
And ask for her favour and call.

How tempting to caress her arm,
Softer than velvet and has charm
In softness like soft glycerine
Or white skin of a beauty queen.

I would kiss her if she agrees
To my fervent and earnest pleas,
And then most happily confess
She has the marks of a goddess.

So does imagination rage
And will not see a different page.
It's fixed on her, light of my eye,
Lovelier than a butterfly.

Play Hard To Get

They said to me, Play hard to get.
I know better; it's of no use.
She is stubborn, her mind is set;
I cannot trick her or abuse.

So what is left that should be done,
Having exhausted my power?
When in the garden shines but one,
Could I pick the choicest flower?

I have offered myself and all.
I cannot offer any more,
But be alone with bitter gall
Biting at me to wound and gore.

Finest Woman

Finest woman of all who live,
How can I honour you?
I will give all that I can give:
My heart and body too.

Will you accept what I bestow
From a meek, earnest heart?
Or will you reject it and throw
The whole or just a part?

Oh, how I relish to shower
Upon you many gifts,
Because I love you every hour,
Unlike the sand that drifts.

Give Me Yourself

You were perplexed as what to give
To cheer my birth and cry to live.
All gifts are water through a sieve.
Give me yourself.

Give me no silver, give no gold;
Give me no treasure, new or old.
Show me no wonders to behold.
Just give yourself.

No diamonds or precious stones,
Ivory or animal bones,
No seats of power and no thrones.
Only yourself.

There is no greater longing for,
Or desire in my very core,
Than loving you, whom I adore.
Give me yourself.

Be done with your vow; marry me.
Open your eyes, and you will see
How wonderful our lives can be.
Give me yourself.

Your Birthday

They all rejoiced when you were born
Just fifty years ago.
A healthy girl like the new morn,
Sweet as a female roe.

'Tis fifty years since you first cried
The cry of the newborn.
You came out wet, but you were dried
And by your mother borne.

I know not how your childhood sped,
And you were truly prized
By a dear man who now is dead.
Now I am tantalized.

You were a fine woman, and lo!
Conquered a lonely heart
Of one whose love did quickly grow—
A furnace from the start.

Oh, how you grew in loveliness,
Completely filled his mind.
And how you showed your comeliness
Of noble, unique kind.

On this, your birthday, I still see
Your loveliness sublime,
Grander than sky and earth and sea,
Unchanged by age or time.

I wish you health and peace within,
Long life and joy each day.
Enjoy your relatives and kin
And think of me someday.

I Saw Her Today

Lord, I saw her today;
My heart was set on fire.
I plead with you and pray,
Help me quench my desire.

Let me not agonize
In the succeeding hours.
I surely recognize
That I lost my powers.

Please help me not to pine
As I have often done.
When pain and hurt were mine,
I found myself undone.

I dreamt of her last night—
A dream of love and joy,
When life was good and bright,
Which we both did enjoy.

Witness how love slew me,
That dangerous domain.
Inspect my heart and see
Hopelessness, love, and bane.

She Walks the Promenade

Fair wind, blow from the Irish Sea,
Caress my love; lovely is she.
Let her spare a small thought for me
As she walks the promenade.

She thinks and ponders when alone,
Reasons and argues on her own.
May thoughts of me be not windblown
As she walks the promenade.

She has a will to persevere
While treading her steps past the pier
On the ground of Cardiganshire,
As she walks the promenade.

When all is done, she walks the road
To her dear home and fair abode.
May she then have removed my load
Having walked the promenade.

I Envy The Birds

Every bit of you is sacred to me:.
Your hands, your feet, and other parts that be
Red rose of Sharon, dearest love, and free,
Splendid woman of the hive, the queen bee.

Life without you is only half a life;
Its inward struggles and longings are rife.
Can a heart filled with love be without strife
When it is broken and cut by your knife?

In this weary world, with its troubles and snares.
I see the crows and the grey doves in pairs.
I envy the birds, and they have no cares—
A dreadful thought that shouts at me and scares.

Spring has returned; its absence was too long.
Time of joy, knowing where one does belong,
The time of loving and love to prolong
The time of loneliness and a fool's song.

The Daffodil

O daffodil by the riverbed,
Why are you bashful now?
Why do you wear a veil that is red
Upon your precious brow?

While sitting, answered the daffodil,
Beside this gentle flood,
A lover's wounded heart did spill
The blood, drenched me with blood.

When Earth Was Young

When Earth was young and heaven blue,
Her love was sweet. But she withdrew,
Leaving a deep hole in my soul:
A broken heart she skinned then slew.

I asked, Is this my lot to be
Alone, with no helpmeet for me,
Living on memories that fade—
Leaves of a deciduous tree?

I walk in a garden of dreams
Where nothing is like what it seems.
Petals adorning the red rose
Are not red petals, but blood streams.

Wounded and cut, without an aid,
I perceived love dwindle and fade
Beyond the edge of no return,
Where it was killed in the dark shade.

She choked my love; it tries to breath
While feelings in great turmoil seethe,
Not knowing which way they should turn
Or whether they should start to wreathe.

Look back and wonder at it all,
How in love there is myrrh and gall,
And things that cannot be resolved
With their deep chasm and great pitfall.

The Computerized Mind

It is a wonder that I find
You made your own home in my mind,
Never to leave or go away
As thoughts of you call me each day.

I wake at night; you come in view.
My thoughts are instantly of you,
Remain until sleep kisses me,
Bids me a night both calm and free.

It is as if my mind is fixed:
Desktop image, always transfixed
Or changed to some other delight
That will give pleasure to my sight.

I find it hard to understand,
When I have not resolved or planned
To think of you or see your face
Or find myself in your embrace.

I do not say, Now think of her,
Think of her figure, of her hair,
Of qualities that gleam and shine,
The ancient Greeks would call divine.

It just happens without my will:
My mind drifts and cannot keep still
To that garden of deepest joy
Where no force can mar or annoy.

My mind must be computerized;
One page has it characterized.
It keeps popping here and there;
Nothing can remove it or tear.

Does She Love You?

They said, "Does she love you well?"
I said, "Maybe, but not enough.
As to how much, I cannot tell,
And find rejection very tough."

"Behave as if you do not care.
Perhaps then she will seek your face."
"It makes no difference; she did swear
To lie in widowhood's embrace.

This is my unfortunate case.
I must bear it and play the man.
All my desires and hopes erase.
This I must try, perhaps I can."

The Joy of Friendship

I fell asleep in her arms.
My mind was fully gratified,
For I was captive to her charms,
And all abuse was nullified.

It was as if the moon had set
His face against the glowing sun
And vowed that he would not forget
The joy of friendship he had won.

But in time, that joy had vanished,
Yet he will forever recall
The bliss that could not be tarnished
When he was sovereign over all.

Hunger

Oh, what hunger, how I languish for lack of bread!
No food to satisfy or raise me from the dead,
But pain and anguish, an empty feeling instead,
With life in the balance held by a cotton thread.

Was it the flood or the drought that caused this to be
A devastated landscape with no crop or tree,
That longs to revive its good life and make it free,
That reserves in its heart a special place for me?

Now, learn this little parable of my sad state,
Which tells that my hunger for you is awesome, great.
Nothing exists to satisfy it or abate,
Except your true love that could open heaven's gate.

Returning Home

The gate of heaven is ajar.
My journey has been long,
For I have travelled from afar
To where I do belong.

The gate of heaven is ajar,
That I may enter in.
Just like a distant shooing star,
But closer to my kin.

What joy, what happiness, what bliss,
Never to stray or roam.
A joy which I did dearly miss
When I was far from home.

Come, fill my cup with happiness
And let me ever drink,
For I have felt the heaviness
When I was near the brink.

How wonderful if I could earn
What I missed ages past.
With sorrow and truth I did learn
Life's pleasures do not last.

One Thought

The mind is full, overflowing.
The thought is one, always gnawing
At my heart's love, ever growing.

O distant dove, will you come back?
My lonely days seem almost black,
Crumbling slowly like an old shack.

Once I beheld her, I was trapped;
In love's domain my soul was wrapped,
And my strong will was quickly sapped.

In that far country I now roam,
Knowing I will never reach home,
Like the shore waves that ebb and foam.

Love's great delights vanished away;
The heart is sick by night and day,
Loath to recover, come what may.

They often said, Such is our life:
A road of sorrow, tears, and strife;
Peace is rare, disappointment rife.

Friendship may last forevermore;
One walks alone outside life's door
Not knowing what life has in store.

Each Day

Each day, the moon floats in the sky.
Each day, the sun burns up on high.
Each day, I think of you and sigh.
I will love you until I die.

O lonely self, how oft you sighed!
How oft you yearned, how oft you tried
To set all works and things aside,
Only to be close by her side!

You are with her, then go away
While your thoughts urge you to dismay.
For you wish you could only stay
Beside her, with her night and day.

Life is too strange; none can explain
The anguish, longings of the brain
That do not vanish but remain
Until we leave this world of pain.

Pining' End

There once was a man who was secure,
Would go through hardships and endure,
Till he saw her and felt compelled
To pursue her and to procure.

But the sea rages, wave on wave;
Volcanoes block their mountain cave
Where men sheltered in ages past
And talked of friends gone who were brave.

Turmoil on turmoil fills the day.
Most would withdraw; the few would stay,
Urging the sun to fill their sky
And chase the snow and cold away.

One year retreats, another comes.
It is easy to add the sums
Of days wasted for evermore
Until to failure he succumbs.

Then he determined not to grieve:
What he missed, he cannot retrieve,
Will stop pining for love denied
From his choicest daughter of Eve.

My Mobile Phone

Every time my mobile phone rings,
My heart misses a beat or two,
Hoping whatever news it brings
Is news that is coming from you.

Then disappointment follows on
When I see text and sender too:
That the message, when it had gone,
Came out upon me from O2.

Trefeddian Hotel

The journey was lovely by car,
The hotel twenty-nine miles far.
On my right sat a shining star.

She brought me here, a birthday treat.
We came to savour lunch and eat.
We chose to have a window seat.

The sea was too near and in sight.
The day was cloudy, but quite bright.
She sat beside me, on my right.

Each had a panini of kind:
Chicken and bacon without rind.
We ate it all, left nought behind.

We then sat back and talked a while.
I learnt mathematics with a smile
From a good teacher without guile.

She Denied Me

She denied me a wondrous bliss,
But what I tell you now is this:
I sorely and painfully miss
Companionship with a woman.

You say, Will any woman do?
Only the one—you know who.
She is the one that I did woo,
Who denied me much happiness.

Is there bitterness in your soul
Towards the one who took and stole
Your heart, affections, and the whole
And left you longing for her love?

Sometimes I ponder, What the hell!
Forget about her and be well.
Her image keeps nagging my shell.
How can I be angry with her?

It is my fault, not hers at all.
I fell for her—and what a fall!
She does excite me and enthral.
Sadly, I must live without her.

Reflections of the Heart

I love you, Sally, very much.
Love to hug you and love to touch.
Love to please you in every way
And much beside, and overmuch.

I could enjoy just every day
To look at you and only say,
How beautiful your features are,
Much fresher than the month of May.

I love you dearly, none beside.
There is no one like you worldwide,
No one to match you anywhere,
In land or sea or countryside.

You, the epitome of your kind,
The loveliest of all mankind,
Lovelier than mountain or sea,
The river, stream, or womankind.

Such are my feelings towards you.
You are fresher than morning dew.
You are forever in my mind,
My heart and soul, and that is true.

She Finished with Me

I will not moan, nor will I cry,
Nor will I wish that I could die,
But I will say with a deep sigh
That she finished with me.

My heart was broken long ago,
Did not recover, remained so.
Until I learn how to let go
Should she finish with me.

I sadly failed to make her mine;
Her love did not reach out to mine.
But I pretended to be fine
When she finished with me.

Who will know the sorrow I feel,
Whether my heart does sway or reel?
I grasped that rejection is real
When she finished with me.

Indeed, I felt totally numb
From head to toe, in arm and thumb,
As if I was of bread a crumb
When she finished with me.

I wished I had a loving friend
Whose love would last until the end,
Until with age, my back will bend.
But she finished with me.

It also came without a word;
No inkling was seen or heard.
She withdrew like a flying bird
When she finished with me.

I feared it would end up like this.
She said goodbye without a kiss.
I must not have any malice
That she finished with me.

I had a close friend at one time
That I thought would be for all time.
When our friendship was in its prime,
He just finished with me.

I still wonder year after year
Why his character was austere,
To cut me off when we were near,
Why he finished with me.

So once again I must relearn
To bear it bravely and not burn.
For what I lost will not return,
Having finished with me.

The End

All the bridges have been broken;
Not one is still standing intact.
No word was heard or was spoken,
For devastation was the fact.

Utter destruction hit the town.
There is no person on the street;
All were ravaged from foot to crown
And were transformed into cold meat.

There is no groaning, no wailing,
No crying in fear or sorrow,
No lamentation, no ailing,
And no one to glimpse the morrow.

No women or babies crying
As fine houses were demolished;
All were either dead or dying.
Observers would be astonished.

No donkey or goat is living,
No dog or cat or bird or fowl.
The shelling was unforgiving;
No creature left to bark or howl.

It was complete devastation
Upon every town and village,
Death checking out every station,
Leaving none to rob or pillage.

This is the story of the town
When disaster trod on its neck.
It was completely broken down
By forces that no one could check.

Oh, my memories of that place!
With joy and sadness, they return,
Reflect the grandeur and the grace
Of one time peace for which I yearn.

Broken Promise

She vowed that she would never wed
After she shared a wedding bed
With her husband who died.
She said I did not lack a thing
And knew my soul to her did cling;
Her promise kept her tied.

She stabbed my heart and may have thought
That I would not mind if she brought
Upon me my demise.
She took the love of a new man
And threw me like a useless can—
That to my great surprise.

For years she protested to me
She and marriage did not agree
Due to her solemn vow.
But this all changed in just a flash,
And I received a great whiplash,
But he a new wife now.

Will you ask me how now I feel
To have to suffer such ordeal
In my adopted land?
The agony, year after year,
Is simply nothing to compare
With this; it seems too bland.

I Felt Betrayed

I felt betrayed, with a big smile,
With no apparent ill or guile.
I just felt betrayed.
Years of friendship fled away;
I had to rue another day
And somehow remain staid.

My heart was grieved too many times,
And I lived through too different climes.
Yet somehow I survived.
Now I lost her and that for good.
I tried and did all that I could;
Believe me, that I strived.

It is useless to moan my fate,
Though my catastrophe is great,
Beyond any control.
Yet still I cannot help myself,
As I have been thrown on the shelf
When she destroyed my soul.

Tell My Mother

Go, tell my mother that her eldest son
By a single woman has been undone.
And in chasing that fair and splendid one,
He hastened to harsh destruction.

Tell her that he bemoans his awful need
For her to marry him and to concede.
But he lost her, and that led with great speed
To another man's attention.

Tell her he is sad and deeply distraught
To learn the lesson that this life has taught:
That one can be a king or can be nought
Due to one, loved to distraction.

See, My Sister

See, my sister, what has happened to me.
I have been robbed of happiness and glee
Because of her rejection.
I shall be lonely with no help to ease
My painful heart that was hot as Hades
Due to her savage action.

Will the morning sun ever smile at me,
Or the bright moon floating in heaven's sea?
Will they ever remember
The joy that I had in her company,
How it became a true testimony
That May turned to December?

I have to live on joyful memory
Of time that was of bliss, a summary,
And not despair and languish.
The fruit tree blossoms, then it is left bare,
The fragrant flowers scented the pure air.
Forsooth, I must not anguish.

Stolen English Rose

English rose in my garden
Of pure exquisite scent,
Should I my large heart harden,
Or should I wail and lament?

You were stolen one morning
Just as the dew appeared.
I felt like crying, mourning,
When you had disappeared.

English rose, now plucked away
By a man of good taste,
I lost you now, and for aye
In seconds and in haste.

No Help

The sea, the blue sea has overwhelmed me.
I am dying, like a stricken bee.
The fierce sharks have attacked and have bit me;
There is no aid and no one to see.

Can anybody help? I cry, Help me,
Save me from this grand awful sea.
Will anyone hear my sad cry and plea?
Lo! No one is standing at the quay.

Farewell this world; I tasted you and knew.
You are subtle with your tricks in view,
Treacherous and not giving any clue.
I perish, die in the ocean blue.

Do not wail, my mother; it was to be
That I perish as I bend the knee
To almighty God, who sets my soul free
From this world of trouble, in the sea.

Broken

Alas! how the jar was broken
And the good wine spilled on the ground.
It was by words that were spoken,
Which are in the English tongue found.

"I am getting married," she said,
When for years she protested nay.
Now her mind was changed and was led
To marry Fred on a near day.

I was broken, devastated,
That thus she turned away from me,
The matter was settled, stated:
Go hang your drum upon the tree.

Marriage

Feel the happiness of the day.
Be glad with us as cows with hay,
Or flowers that blossom in May.
But I shall not be there.

It is right now a month in spring
When joyous hearts rejoice and sing
The beauty that this world does bring.
But I shall not be there.

Partake with us in church and eat
To celebrate this noble feat.
See the proud guests and let friends meet.
But I shall not be there.

It is a rite which God ordained,
When man at first his wife obtained.
All are glad and nothing is strained.
But I shall not be there.

See the bridegroom kiss the bride.
See him carry himself with pride
In this, our town by the seaside.
But I shall not be there.

Goodbye

Goodbye, my love. You did me wrong.
You sold me quickly for a song.
I always hoped, always did long
That you would marry me.

Forsooth, indeed, you made your choice.
It was not I to hear your voice.
My longing done, I would rejoice
If you had married me.

But life cheats us and does not mind
If we are happy or go blind.
It has been cruel and unkind:
You did not marry me.

Your new husband was greatly pleased
That you chose him; his heart was eased.
But I remain as one diseased,
When you did not wed me.

The Thunderbolt of Zeus

When Earth was young and heaven blue,
I never thought and never knew
That I would be battered and shred
And cooked like potatoes and stew.

I thought I found a companion,
A kind woman, not a stallion.
But she left me and went her way,
Alone in a rugged canyon.

It was one day, when all was fine,
That my beloved did undermine
The hope I had in heart and mind.
I have to a new life resign.

She hit me with a thunderbolt
That would cause any horse to bolt,
And added that she made a choice
That gave my heart a sudden jolt.

That she will be no longer mine,
But another's by a firm sign
Which she experienced on the way
That made her sure it was divine.

She thus blew out my eager flame
And would take another man's name,
Left me to struggle with some thoughts
That I know well from whence they came.

The Good Shepherd Giveth His Life for the Sheep
John 10:11

I would have given my life for her
If the dire need be,
And all my goods to her transfer
If she'd married me.

But she went from me and left me
In deep agony.
She closed the door and took the key
Of matrimony.

The magpie came upon the tree
As I wrote these words;
It was alone and just like me
Lone amongst the birds.

She Never Said I Love You

She never told me, "I love you,"
Though I said it many a time.
She let me hug and kiss her too,
And that was so for quite some time.

But now I see and fully know
That it meant nothing, was not true.
She dumped me now and will bestow
Her whole body to someone new.

She gave her kisses, but not love,
To me when I asked her to be
My wife, well honoured, a true love.
She will be that to him, not me.

I count my loss now every day
And cannot keep her out of mind.
May God help me that soon I may
Accept, forget, leave her behind.

They Asked

They asked, Why have you abandoned the meeting?
I answered, It is too much for me to bear,
To look on her face and feel my heart beating
As she sits happily with another there.

They said, You will overcome this hurt in time.
You surely will learn to forgive and forget,
Whether in this town or in another clime.
Time is a healer for those caught in the net.

I said, I am like a wounded animal
That needs solitude and peace so that it heals.
This is the least to have and is minimal
To withstand all life's burdens, its wounds and weals.

Tell My Brother

Tell me, brother, whom can I trust
After what befell me this year?
My closest friend let me eat dust,
Though she is matchless and most dear.

Are women fickle? I must say
Some are, some are faithful to death.
It is my misfortune to lay
On her my trust, my life, my breath.

After much agony and hurt,
I am being restored to live.
Rather than lying in the dirt,
Must rise and practice to forgive.

Too sad, it cannot be undone.
No use to groan, useless to moan.
I have lost her, the only one
For whom I longed, now not my own.

God's Blessings

Let me not grieve for my great loss,
For in this life there is much dross.
But let the joy tunes come across
As I count my blessings.

They are too many every day;
They come to me and make me say,
Thank the good Lord now and alway;
He is rich in blessings.

His countenance on me does fall
Despite the doubts that will befall,
For he is kind and does enthral
My soul with his blessings.

Learn of my case, all of mankind.
Our God is love, and he is kind.
Learn in your grief, take it to mind:
God endows his blessings.

Ah, Beloved Woman

Ah! beloved woman of one man,
How could you marry another
When I loved you as best I can,
With love exceeding all other?

Excelling the love of all men,
I wooed you and asked you to be
My wife, whom I would cherish then
And grant all your wishes from me.

But time went on, and the fruit fell
Not in my garden, but in yours.
And I could not fathom or tell
How closeness died behind closed doors.

Behind closed doors, I sit alone
And think of happy days gone by,
With every nerve and every bone
Within my body, asking, Why?

My Love for You

You went from me; I love you still.
I cannot get my heart to dry.
My feelings live; I fail to kill
One small inkling and let it die.

You now became a wife to him.
My love for you will not perish;
It thrives and overflowed the brim
While he is your own to cherish.

Love another man's wife? How strange
A thing for me that I should do.
Perhaps God will help me to change,
Perhaps will dull my love for you.

Can Love Turn into Hate?

Can my love turn into hate,
Or will it try to ornate
My inner self?
I hoped I could activate
True love in her to permeate
Her inner self.

The years failed to make her change,
And I found it very strange
Within myself
That she would never exchange
Love, as it was out of range
Within herself.

Thus it was and thus would stay;
Our friendship would go astray
Between ourselves,
For she kept herself at bay
And my longing heart would slay,
Did this herself.

The Stricken Heart

The sun is shining brightly now.
My heart is sad, ready to bow
To utter despair.
I must not listen to its call;
Nothing should hurt me or enthral,
And my will impair.

Will a heart stricken, smitten hard
Mend or just melt like soft lard?
It will surely mend.
Arrows of love were far too fierce,
But rejection does prick and pierce,
More so from a friend.

Nothing pains me, nothing does stir,
Than knowing he is loving her
In the proper way.
I fail to keep this out of mind.
The thought assaults me and does grind
All the joys of day.

Will I in time be strong enough
To let such thoughts go and such stuff?
I will, but not now.
My days roll on from light to night.
I want to get rid of such blight
That ails me, but how?

May the good Lord listen to me,
Ease my heart pain by great degree,
And I shall be glad.
I ask that he will do it soon
Before many a day and noon
Bid me not be sad.

I Saw Her Today

I saw her today,
And did my heart stay
Sober and unmoved?
Yes, I say it did,
And it did not skid.
Of this I approved.

We walked a short way.
Kept myself at bay
And deemed her precious.
Quite pleased with myself.
She was her true self,
And she looked luscious.

Joyous excitement,
Pleasant enticement
Would melt my heart.
But she is not mine.
Hence I did not pine,
Nor in a way smart.

May it remain so,
For I truly know
My pain has been great.
And I mind that she
Belongs not to me.
My storm must abate.

The Net

I cannot stop loving her.
The net is strong and well weaved.
I was caught up in the lair
Of her love, to which I cleaved.

I now have to free myself,
Be again myself once more.
No hurt can come to one's self
If his life he can restore.

Where is my knife? I may cut
Those bands holding me too tight.
The door is only half shut
To freedom into the night.

Thus it was a tale once told
Of a man enslaved by ropes
Who was clever and too bold,
Who escaped against all hopes.

Oblivious

She is oblivious of my plight
And thinks that my sorrow is slight.
Because I show not that I grieve,
She finds it too hard to perceive.

She thinks matters are as before,
But hurting and pain bite and gore.
She does assume that all is well
And that I have survived the swell.

I do not show how hurt I am
When I was struck down by a tram.
Behave like one who never lost
A thing, I say, of worthy cost.

But she was worth the world to me
And grander than the grand blue sea,
More beautiful to my eyesight
Than Venus in the sky at night.

We Talk

We talk together on the phone
When each of us is home alone.
I do not moan, whine, or complain,
As if I am no more in pain.

But that is falsehood on my part.
I do not see why I should start
To tell all that is in my soul,
As if I need her to console.

Such is the state between us two.
I do not plead with her or woo,
For she dumped me and closed the door
And left me writhing on the floor.

A story is known that one man
Was ostracized by his own clan.
But he somehow managed to live,
Feeding on pain that life does give.

I Had Such Love

She was a pleasant friend to me,
But slipped away and let me see
Loneliness in turmoil.
She found a different spouse who will
Love and protect her from all ill.
My heart is on the boil.

How had she acted such a deed
When I seek for comfort and need
To be loved and embraced?
But life is treacherous, unkind.
She, of women, should really mind
How I sought her and chased.

Life is too short and very brief.
Some men do know happy relief
When held by a dear wife.
And I had such love long ago,
But I lost her with a fierce blow.
There is none in my life.

The Hammer of Thor

The great hammer of Thor
Hammered me with a blow.
For one, I do adore,
Did her strong power show.

She struck me in my heart,
My soul, my mind, and all,
And let me break apart,
Hard pierced by her awl.

I fell upon the ground
Bleeding, ashen, dismayed,
Not making any sound
As I struggled, betrayed.

She smashed me with great force,
Let me just writhe with pain,
She feeling slight remorse
While I lost all my gain.

The Sea Storm

The fierce storm has abated,
Not one second belated,
And the ship did not drift down.
The sea, with its furore,
Had shown its awesome glory
And power of great renown.

The journey should now proceed;
The sailing is calm indeed
And no longer boisterous.
Let us arrive safely home.
We have seen abundant foam
When the sea was treacherous.

See our loved ones and rejoice,
And speak with jubilant voice
That we are at last secure.
For our journey gave us all
The fear of death and a fall
Into the wider azure.

The Church Walk

They walk by the seashore,
Fifteen persons or more,
Upon the promenade
But do not get footsore.

Their pace, for her, is slow,
Slower than the black crow.
Walks again at her pace,
An arrow from the bow.

She tries to keep her weight
Too little and not great.
But she is not obese,
Yet quickly speeds her gait.

She is lovely, demure,
With a figure to lure
The heart of any man.
And mine was one for sure.

Her Birthday

It is her birthday today.
I wished her a happy day,
Remembered the years of yore.
How they have vanished for aye.

I sent to her a small gift,
Not to heal the broken rift
That came between us and said,
Your friendship has gone adrift.

She texted me, "I am touched."
Not that she felt that I clutched
To a trick which made her feel
That my longings are retouched.

I wish her every blessing
In her life and everything.
Although I shall not be there,
Wished her a happy wedding.

Thus life goes by, and I still
Heed my affections and will
Love her till the day I die,
Love her much against my will.

Is it a wrong thing to love
One who was my only love?
Who now has another man
But was once my turtledove?

My Jewel

I lost my jewel. Where has it gone?
Some man has found it, and he has won.
His gain my loss, his joy my sadness;
Mine the sore regret, his the gladness.

I searched for another, but there was none.
My diamond is the only one.
Nothing can match it; someone may say
I have found a rare jewel this day.

They say, Do not cry over spilled milk.
But what if it drenched the purest silk?
There is cause for sorrow, cause for pain.
My loss is permanent, someone's gain.

But time heals the wounds that it has made,
The wounds that bled and for a time stayed.
Life must go on, but not as before.
My loss, sorrow, and many things more.

Night Musings, After The End Came

I sorely hurt, woefully grieve,
For I loved her beyond compare
And find it too hard to perceive
My love has sought comfort elsewhere.

What is a greater woe beside
A place in hell, there to abide?
A broken friendship, fractured, torn
When she at once left me forlorn.

It is as if the waves overwhelmed me
And brought me down to perish and to die.
I felt the tightness in my breast crush me
And thought that I should never see the sky.

I felt that I was cheated.
Too late—it is completed.
She is happy with her life,
But I am sad, defeated.

People do what they want and call it God's will.

Rejection is final, complete;
There is no reprieve or relief.
I reaped great loss and sore defeat,
Must not harbour malice or grief.

How could you betray me?
How could you do it?
Years of friendship with me
Did not count one whit.

Night Musings, Before the End

Pure nectar flowed from your lips.
When I drank, I was vivified
From the fountain that never dried
Each time I tasted your sweet lips.

I never knew if she ever loved me;
She did not tell me or imply.
My love for her overwhelmed me
And will persist until I die.

It is broken, it is broken.
O wretched man, it is broken,
All hope is lost, all remedies.
My heart, my heart, it is broken.

I sorely missed her company
And spent my days lonely, alone,
Knowing the heart and agony
Of an orphan bereft, forlorn.

She hurt me grievously,
Wounded me deeply,
And slew me mercilessly,
Yet I love her still.

When Earth was young and heaven blue,
The evening sky a dark red hue,
A voice was heard, a cry of pain:
I am incomplete without you.

It hurts to live on memories,
For they engender miseries,
And joy was not reborn.
Delights of yesteryear are gone,
The heart's shroud with white lace was spun,
Is ready to be worn.

You never knew how much I loved you,
More than the sea waves for the shore,
The moon and its ancient folklore,
The Earth's beauty and fiery core,
The eagle's zeal to fly and soar.
More than the sun's zest to set west,
The red robin for its own nest,
The beating heart in my own chest,
The suckling baby for the breast.
More than diamonds and their worth,
More than all things upon this earth.

Man without a woman
Is like a house without foundations,
Like a sun without sunlight,
Like a body without a soul.

My lonely heart, it wails and cries.
It wants her love; for her it sighs.
It cannot get what it longs for,
Cannot forget her love before.

Upon this day, a babe was born.
She grew to be fairer than morn,
Fairer than sea, red sky, or moon.
They called her Sally.

I wish she'd let me kiss her.

She gave a hug, but not a kiss;
A second best, not higher bliss.
Leaving a sad tormented soul
Pining for that which went amiss.

POSTMORTEM

Written before she decided to marry

Dearest Sally,

By the time you read this, I would have gone home.

I loved you dearly and unceasingly, and despite my pretence, I never stopped longing for you.

Goodbye, my love.

See you at the Resurrection.

If only!

Salim

Printed in the United States
By Bookmasters